Trench Ballads & Other Verses by Erwin Clarkson Garrett

Index Of Poems

PREFACE

I have divided this book into three distinct parts. Part I, Trench Ballads, consists of forty American soldier poems of America's participation in the World War, 1917-19, based entirely on actual facts and incidents, and almost exclusively on my own personal experiences and observations, when a private in Company G, 16th Infantry, First Division, of the American Expeditionary Forces in France. Part II, Pre-war Poems, consists of three sets of verses written just before the active entry of America in the war, and appertaining to, but not an integral part of, it, and therefore grouped separately. Part III, Other Poems, contains those of a general and non-military character.

It is highly desirable the "Notes" at the end of this volume should be consulted, and that it be realized that with few exceptions, all these Trench Ballads were written in France, many scribbled on odd pieces of paper or on old envelopes in the trenches themselves, and consequently, when present locality is intimated, it is always France, that is to say, from the standpoint that I am speaking in and from the seat of operations. For example, when I use the term "over here," it really means what the people at home in America would call "over there." Hyperbole or little characteristic anecdotes that really never occurred, except in the brain of an author, I have absolutely shunned, and have endeavored to adhere strictly to "the truth, the whole truth and nothing but the truth," and to set forth the vicissitudes; the dangers, joys and tribulations of the army man, and especially the man in the ranks, and more especially the man in the ranks of the Infantry, as these latter formed the actual front-line or combat troops that bore the brunt in this greatest of all wars.

Absolute continuity or sequence would seem superfluous, but it will be observed that I have endeavored to maintain it to a certain extent, i.e., by gradually leading from a number of military verses, without any strict inter-relation, to the day of being wounded, then on to several poems concerning the military hospital, and finally bringing the Trench Ballads to a close with those having to do with the returning home of the soldier.

My previous book, "Army Ballads and Other Verses," is the result of my experiences when serving as a private in Companies "L" and "G," 23rd Infantry and Troop "I," 5th Cavalry (Regulars), during the Philippine Insurrection of 1899-1902, and if "Army Ballads and Other Verses" is taken in conjunction with this volume, it is my hope together they may prove a fairly comprehensive anthology of the American soldier of recent times.

E. C. G.

Philadelphia,
November 1st, 1919.

MY COMRADES IN THE RANKS.

You chose no easy Service,
No safe job, friends of mine,
But the mud of the shell-torn, trenches
And the foremost battle-line.
No camouflage patriotism
Though you had from a wealth to choose
But the wicked work of No Man's Land,
Filling a man's-size shoes.

You didn't say you wouldn't play
If you got no shoulder bars
You even placed your Country
Above a general's stars:
For shocking, very shocking,
You didn't give a damn
About your "social status,"
When you fought for Uncle Sam.

Friends of mine, friends of mine,
I've shared your toil and tears
Your dangers and your little woes,
When days were turned to years.
I may not make them understand
The things that you have done,
But God bless you and God keep you
Every blessed mother's son.

PART I. TRENCH BALLADS.

TRENCHES.

Trenches dripping, wet and cold
Trenches hot and dry
Long, drab, endless trenches
Stretching far and nigh.

Zigzag, fretted, running sere
From the cold North Sea,
'Cross the muddy Flanders plain
And vales of Picardy.

Through the fields of new, green wheat

Filled with poppies red,
While abandoned plow-shares show
Whence the peasants fled.

Past the great cathedral towns,
Where each gorgeous spire
Torn and tottering, slowly wilts
'Neath the Vandals' ire.

Hiding in the shadows
Of the hills of French Lorraine,
And bending south through rugged heights
To the land of sun again.

Trenches, endless trenches,
Shod with high desire
All that man holds more than life,
And touched with patriot fire.

Trenches, endless trenches,
Where tightening draws the cord
'Round the throat of brutal Kultur,
And its red and dripping sword.

Trenches, endless trenches,
Bleached and choked with rain,
Could ye speak what tales ye'd tell
Of honor, death and pain.

Could ye speak, what tales ye'd tell
Of shame and golden worth,
To the glory and damnation
Of the spawn of all the Earth.

BARB-WIRE POSTS.
Five o 'clock; the shadows fall
In mist and gloom and cloud;
And No Man's Land is a sullen waste,
Wrapped in a sodden shroud;
And the click of Big Mac's moving foot
Is a dangerous noise and loud.

Ten o'clock; the wind moans low
Each tree is a phantom gray:
And the wired posts are silent ghosts
That move with a drunken sway;
(But never a gleam in No Man's Land
Till the dawn of another day).

Twelve o 'clock; the heavens yawn

Like the mouth of a chasm deep;
And see—that isn't the fence out there
It's a Boche—and he stoops to creep
I'll take a shot—oh hell, a post
(Oh God, for a wink o' sleep).

Two o 'clock; the cold wet fog
Bears down in dripping banks:
Ah, here they come—the dirty hounds
In swinging, serried ranks!
Why don't the automatics start? . . .
Or do my eyes play pranks?

It doesn't seem a column now,
But just two sneaking there:
And one is climbing over,
While the other of the pair
Is clipping at the wires
With exasperating care.

(I'm sober as a gray-beard judge
I'm calm as the morning dew
I'm wide awake and I'll stake
My eyes with the best of you;
But I can't explain just how or why
Posts do the things they do.)

Three o'clock; they're on the move
Well, let the beggars come. . . .
A crash — a hush — a spiral shriek
And a noise like a big bass drum
(I hope that Hun shot hasn't found
Our kitchen and the slum).

Five o'clock; the first faint streak
Of a leaden dawn lifts gray;
And the barb-wire posts are sightless ghosts
That swagger, click and sway,
And seem to grin, in their blood-stained sin,
In a most unpleasant way.

FEET.
Some say this war was fought and won
With gleaming bayonets,
That lift and laugh with Death's own chaff
And leave no fond regrets:
Some, by the long lean foul-lipped guns
Where the first barrages meet,
But I, by the poor old weary limping
Tired broken feet.

Some say this war was fought and won
By the crawling, reeking gas;
Some, by the flitting birdmen,
That dip and pause and pass:
Some, by the splitting hand-grenades
But I, I hear the beat
Of the poor old faithful worn limping
Tired broken feet.

Some say the war was fought and won
By This or That or Those
But I, by heel and sunken arch
And blistered, bleeding toes.
Drag on, drag on, oh weary miles,
Through mire, slush and sleet,
To the glory of the rhythm
Of the poor old broken feet.

YOUR GAS-MASK.

When over your shoulders your "full-field" you fling,
And you curse the whole load for a horrible thing,
What is it you reach for, as outward you swing?
Your gas-mask.

If you head for a bath by the small river's flow
Though only a distance of fifty or so
What is it you carefully grab ere you go?
Your gas-mask.

When in full marching-order, where mules might suffice,
And you count your equipment, each having its price,
What is it you feel for and count over twice?
Your gas-mask.

In morning and afternoon, evening and night
In first or support lines, in sleep or in fight,
What is it you cherish and cling to so tight?
Your gas-mask.

What is it you never leave thoughtless behind?
What is it you clutch for with fingers that bind
As you sniff that first odor that comes on the wind?
Your gas-mask.

SLUM AND BEEF STEW.

It's a lot of dirty water
And some little dabs of spuds,
And dubious hunks of gristly meat

And divers other duds.

Served up to us in trenches,
Our hunger made it good,
But elsewhere—when we got it
"We ate it, if we could.

And now about the time Josephus
Tells his gobs to call
Port and Starboard, left and right,
We're ordered, one and all,

To most respectfully address
Our slum as "beef stew"—Gosh,
Methinks the Brains of the Army
Has dished-up awful bosh.

For slum is slum, and your Tummy-tum
Has called it so for aye;
As 'twas when Thotmes III marched north
To check the Hittites' sway.

As 'twas when Cyrus' doughboys swept
Through the Cilician Gates
And as 'twill ever be so long
As a weary mess-line waits.

So long as Nations fight and eat
Though all don't feed as well
For the Colonel is Sitting on the World
While we are S. O. L.

Perhaps, kind friend, our logic may
Strike you as on the bum
But as we're Pershing's slum-hounds,
We'll call the damn thing "slum".

SHELL-FIRE.
The Hun he taught us Gas and things
But the high explosive shell
Was born of the Devil's mirth
And the reddest forge in Hell.

Now one hits the village church,
And the ancient, wavering wall
And the little pointed tower swing
And stagger and sway and fall.

Now one hits a red-slag roof,
And eighty feet on high

Towers a monstrous, salmon cloud
Against an azure sky.

Now one hits in a field of wheat,
Fresh planted, fair and green,
And a mighty, thundering crater bursts
Where abandoned plows careen.

Now one nears with spiral shriek
And strikes in the long white road,
And the Lord ha' mercy on the Red Cross truck,
And its helpless, weary load.

Now one comes where you crouching wait
In the trench's far-flung line,
And you know there is never shelter against
The voice of that deadly whine.

Now one pierces the dugout's roof,
And when the foul smokes pass,
What once was there a dozen men
Is a crimson, clotted mass.

In the pale moonlight or the black of night
When the sunset fires flare
In the noontime's calm, without alarm,
The Great Arch Fiend is there,
With his frightful cry as he rushes nigh
On his errand of despair.

MR. FLY.

There's a nice stiff breeze ablowing,
Mr. Fly;
That keeps from out my trench.
The decomposing stench
Of a soldier, Boche or French,
Mr. Fly.

So please run off and play,
Mr. Fly.
So please run off and play
Like a good fly, right away,
For I want to sleep today,
Mr. Fly.

I'm dozing like a bull-finch,
Mr. Fly,
When you hop me, unaware,
And I wake and swat and swear,
And you return with thoughtful care,

Mr. Fly.

Can't you see I'm very tired,
Mr. Fly?
That the G. I. Cans don't bust,
And I've nibbled on a crust,
And deserve a snooze, I trust,
Mr. Fly.

Do you think it's square and decent,
Mr. Fly,
When the Cooties cease to bite,
(And there is no sleep at night)
That you give me no respite,
Mr. Fly?

An hour's calm is with us,
Mr. Fly;
And the endless battle strain,
And the shelling and the rain,
Ought to make it very plain,
Mr. Fly

That I need a little nap,
Mr. Fly.
That I do need mighty well
Just to sun and rest a spell,
And to sleep here where I fell,
Mr. Fly.

So have a heart, oh have a heart!
Mr. Fly.
If you're looking for a fight
And you must come 'round and bite,
Make your visit in the night,
Mr. Fly.

THE SALVATION ARMY WITH THE A. E. F.

You kept no roped-off rows of chairs
Or clubs "For Officers Only,"
But you toiled for John Doe when he was
Cold, tired, wet and lonely.

You didn't squander millions
On soldiers warming benches,
But you worked like blazes for the ones
That frequented the trenches.

You didn't stick to cast-iron rules
Of business most punctilious,

And you never treated Private Doe
With manner supercilious.

You had no boundless backing
But just inside your doors
It seemed like, "Feel to home, Bill
Sit down, the place is yours."

Some things we fain remember
Some things we fain forget
But you, oh kindly people,
Live in our memory yet.

SHELL-HOLES.

They're ugly, jagged, cone-shaped holes
That litter up the ground,
That ruin all the landscape
For miles and miles around.

That pock-mark fertile fields of green
That rip the hard French roads,
And catch the lumbering trucks at night
Agroan beneath their loads.

And some of them are little uns
The shrill one-pounders plow
About a meter—edge to edge
But large enough, I trow.

And some of them nigh twice as broad,
And rather more straight down,
The "77" Boches' gift,
Of dubious renown.

And some of them a dozen feet
From rim to ragged rim,
And deep enough to hide a horse
A crater, gaunt and grim.

And some of them are yellow-black,
Where clings the reek of gas,
(But here we do not pause to gaze,
Nor linger as we pass).

And some of them are water-fouled
Or dried and parched and dun;
And some of them are newly turned
Fresh blotches 'neath the sun.

But all spell red destruction,

Blind rage and blinding hate,
To them who charge the shell-swept zone
Or in the trenches wait.

Should we say "all," or modify
Our statement? Any fool
Knows that exceptions always rise
To prove an iron-clad rule.

And so in this case we can name
Some shell-holes we have met,
The thought of whose engulfing sides
Clings in our memory yet.

They were the holes we rolled into
When iron or bullet struck
Cursing the cursed Prussian,
And blessing our blesséd luck.

Oh lovely, beauteous shell-hole,
Wherein we helpless lay,
A wondrous couch of velvet
Ye seemed to us that day.

Our blood it stained your cushions
A deep and richer red,
As shrieking messengers of death
Sped harmless overhead.

Swept whining in their blood-lust,
Hell's music, bleak and grim,
Splitting in rage the edges
Of your all-protecting rim.

Oh shell-holes, murderous shell-holes,
In vales of grass and wheat
On hillside and in forest,
In road and village street

Your toll of suffering and death
Is flashed to East and West
But tell they of the wounded
Ye've sheltered in your breast?

FOOD.
We've eaten at the Plaza, at Sherry's and the Ritz
The Bellevue and the Willard and the Ponce de Leon too.
We've sampled all the cooking of the Savoy and Meurice,
Through a palate-tickling riot that Lucullus never knew.

From tables where the Northern Fires greet the coming night—
To Raffles out in Singapore and the Palace in Bombay;
From Shepheard's (which means Cairo) to that little hostelry
Way down in Trinchinopoly where purring punkahs sway.

We've traveled north, we've traveled south by all routes known to man—
We've traveled east, we've traveled west by some they scarcely came:
From canvasback and terrapin to Russian caviar,
From venison to bird-nest soup and curried things and game.

We've put them all beneath our belt with consummate address:
We've risen from the laden board and smacked our jowl in glee.
With organs sound and healthy we have murdered each menu
And left the wreck of good things with a gourmet's ecstasy.

But do you wish to know the feasts that permeated deep—
That stirred the very bottom of my stomach to the core?
Quisine that brought such wondrous bliss, but satiated
not, That saturating satisfied, but still left room for more?

The place—a little half deserted town in northern France:
The time—a time of carnage, of wanton strife and hate:
And I and my battalion on reserve a week or two
Till they call us to the Front again to force the hands of Fate.

Just from the Commissary, the Salvation or the Y,
I've got a bar of chocolate, some butter and some cake;
A canteen full of milk, and eggs, from the old farmhouse near by,
And with this tout ensemble you can see I'm sitting jake.

I've entered now a peasant's house—an ancient, kindly dame—
Who's seen me several times before, and knows just what I wish:
So the frying-pan is gotten out—the pewter fork and
knife— A big bowl and the skillet and a large, substantial dish.

And I'm breaking up the bar of chocolate in a mighty bowl
(The while the eggs are frying, "Sur le plat, oui, s'il vous plait"),
And pouring from my canteen's gurgling mouth a draught of milk,
To expedite proceedings in a purely tactful way.

And now the spluttering eggs are done, the chocolate's hot and rich;
I have my feet beneath the board, the pewter weapons near:
A hunger from a front-line trench—the stomach of a goat—
And a battle-line that's very far, though still the guns ring clear.

And thus, too full for utterance, I gently draw the veil—
So leave me, kindly reader, in my joy—
And maybe you will understand why other dinners pale,
And in comparison with this, appear to clog and cloy.

We've soldiered many, many moons
In this old plugging war,
And all the ills and all the thrills,
We've had 'em o'er and o'er.

Shell-fire, G. I. Cans and Gas
Night work in No Man's Land
And everything that calls for nerve,
Endurance, guts and sand.

We've argued which we liked the worst
Machine-guns, gas or shell.
We've ruminated carefully
And done it rather well.

And after all our resumé
And cogitating bull,
We've reached a clear decision,
Most amplified and full:

The greatest time in all the life
Of any living man
The mightiest moment of the Game
The proudest, high élan;

The thing we came three thousand miles
Across the seas to do
"The Day," the splendid hour
That waits for me and you,

Arrives—We spring into the wastes
Of land, ripped, roweled and barred
The battle-lust in brain and eye
The weary jaw set hard;

The rifle gripped in hands of steel,
Where, flashing in the sun,
Sweep on our blazing bayonets,
The terror of the Hun.

THE BATTLE MOTHER
Over the sodden trenches
Over the skirmish line
High o'er the hole-torn fields and roads
Cometh a face to mine.

Under the burning gas attack,
And the stench of the bursting shell,
We hope we may live for her dear sake

She who would wish us well.

(She who has ever cherished us
But when the hour came
Choked back the tears of the faithful years,
As we left to play the game.)

Between the blazing horizons
That hammer the long night through,
Lapping their tongues of hatred
Fearless she comes to you.

And over the roar of battle
Where the shrill-voiced shrapnel sings,
Shine forth the loving eyes we hold
Above all earthly things.

A World run mad with slaughter
A charnel-house of blood
But the face of the Battle Mother
Above the crimson flood.

SONG OF THE VOLUNTEERS OF 1917
The drafted men fought hard and well,
The whole big army did,
But we prefer the spirit
Of the Bayard and the Cid.

The drafted men fought hard and well,
But when Jack sailed for France,
They didn't have to drag us in
By the back of our neck and the seat of our pants.

The drafted men fought hard and well,
But when it first began,
From coast to coast, from Lakes to Gulf,
We rose, a single man.

The drafted men fought hard and well,
But when the days were black,
Glad we sprang to the call to front
The snarling, charging pack.

The red-fanged, savage hounds of hate,
In a victor's drunken might:
The unleashed, howling gray hordes
Sweeping plain and height.

The drafted men fought hard and well,
But when the great floes pressed,

Came we to break the ice and clear
A channel for the rest.

The drafted men fought hard and well,
But now the thing is o'er,
We 're glad we came the way we came
When the Nation rose to war.

The drafted men fought hard and well,
But now the thing is done,
We're glad we came the time we came
In the heyday of the Hun.

Shades of Patrick Henry
Of Washington and Hale,
God grant we've kept the trust—God grant
The Old Guard shall not fail.

The drafted men fought hard and well,
The whole vast army did,
But we prefer the spirit
Of the Bayard and the Cid.

O. D.

O. D., it ought to mean Oh Damn,
When in the pay of Uncle Sam:
But when you hear the soldier blab
"O. D.," it just means Olive Drab.

The leggings, breeches and the boots
Of Uncle Samuel's war galoots
The overcoats and jackets too,
Confess the selfsame mournful hue.

It may be excellent camouflage
To try to fool a young barrage;
It may not show the bally dirt
So much upon your knees and shirt.

It may be serviceable and such
When you are beating-up the "Dutch;"
But from a calm esthetic point,
The color's sadly out-of-joint.

A little mud on red or blue
May seem quite prominent to you;
But put the same upon O. D.,
And the whole blame thing looks mud to me.

But then, it matches trenches well,

And things that make you say, Oh Hell
For instance, hikes, inspections, drills,
And busted arms with C. C. pills.

It makes you heave a sigh or two
For the good old days of brass and blue;
But if it's fit to beat the "Dutch"
I guess it doesn't matter much.

ARTILLERY REGISTERING

They're shooting shrapnel o'er the trench
My boy.
They're shooting shrapnel o'er the trench,
Which means tonight they'll surely drench
These works with shells that burst and stench
(And cloy).

They're shooting shrapnel o'er the trench
My lad.
It breaks with shrill and tinny sound,
And quite promiscuously around
It showers metal on the ground
(It's bad).

They're shooting shrapnel o'er the trench
Recruit.
So do not stand and stupid stare
Till some comes down and parts your hair,
But hunt your dugout and beware
(To boot).

They're shooting shrapnel o'er the trench
Young man.
Which means tonight the gas shells' thud
Will muffled fall like chunks of mud;
And th' blinding, crashing Prince of Blood
The G. I. Can.

They're shooting shrapnel o'er the trench
My child.
And ere the dawn is turning gray
You mark the very words I say
There's going to be hell to pay
(High piled).

RECIPROCITY

We haven't been in this large strife
So very long to date,
But we have learned our answer to

The Prussian "Hymn of Hate."
And we are feeding him for pap,
As plain as A. B. C,
A pretty little ditty known
As "Reciprocity."

The Hun he planned for War, red War,
By ocean, air and land;
And he is getting oodles of
The same, to date, in hand.
He suddenly sprang poison gas
Upon a valiant foe,
And now he's getting gas and gas,
And more gas, as you know.

He found new tricks and wrinkles for
This gory battle game,
And now we stoop, no more his dupe,
And beat him at the same.
He drowned our women in the sea—
He ravished where he won—
But these were little things we couldn't
Copy from the Hun.

His crimson heel lie bade us feel,
His lust and pride and scorn—
Till, echoing in our weary breasts
A righteous hate was born. . . . .
Beware the patient man in wrath,
The olden proverb saith;
And, Spawn of a Kultur nursed in blood
In blood meet ye your death.

TRUCKS

Lunging-wild, careening trucks
Plunging through the rain,
Sweeping down the rainbow road
To the sunlit plain.
And echoing back with ponderous roar
Their cargo's wild refrain.

We're bowling over the roads of France
White roads.
We're twenty gray tracks in a long, long line,
Twisting and rumbling and feeling fine.
And someday we'll roll to the Watch on the Rhine
Joyous loads.

But now we're returning to billets for rest
Earned repose.

We've been in the trenches for many a week.
In rain and in wind and in dugouts that leak.
Till we all are so hoarse we scarcely can speak.
Goodness knows.

Our clothes they are worn and tattered and torn,
And mud?
My heavens! we have it in our leggings and hair
On breeches and jackets and all that we wear
But we are so happy, we really don't care
'Tisn't blood.

It isn't those long, endless vigils at night,
On the rack.
It isn't the fighting and hunger and heat
It isn't the slush and rheumatics and sleet
It isn't the once-a-day cold meal we eat
In the black.

It isn't the shelling from sun unto sun
Curséd shells:
It isn't the camouflage that you must use
If you have to lie down in your trench for a snooze,
It isn't the stenches the Hun corpses choose
For their smells.

But it's clean clothes and gasoline-bath and a shave
What a treat!
It's sleeping on elegant straw, and undressed,
With never a Toto disturbing your rest;
It's regaining your "pep" and a wonderful zest
When you eat.

We're all of us willing, we're all of us game
For the fray:
But now we have finished a good hitch, and more,
In conducting this large and salubrious war,
Do you think we should feel very tearful or sore
On this day?

So some we are singing and some shoot the bull,
And some sleep.
(Don't wake the poor devil, just leave him alone,
Though he's jammed on your foot till it's dead as a
stone),
And we rumble through towns on the way to our own,
Packed like sheep.

And your hand is afingering bills large and small
Francs galore.
And you've visions of things that your poor stomach begs,

Including nuts, candy and chocolate and eggs;
And you find you've forgotten the crick in your legs
Cramped and sore.

We're a light-hearted, dirty-faced, rollicking crew
Grimy pawed:
Though a few cogitate on the living and dead,
And some look behindward, and some look ahead,
And some think of bunkies that shrapnel has sped
To their God.

Lunging-wild, careening trucks
Plunging through the rain,
Sweeping down the rainbow road
To the sunlit plain,
And echoing back with ponderous roar
Their cargo's wild refrain.

MADEMOISELLE

Oh Mademoiselle behind the Lines,
When we're weary and covered with dirt,
And you make a promenade with us,
Or perhaps you mend our shirt.

You know our lives from your brothers,
Or your sweethearts who can't come back,
But only your laughter greets us
When we shed that awful "pack."

And some of you sell eggs to us
In a town whence most have fled:
And some of your names have "de" and your blood
Runs blue as well as red.

Oh Mademoiselle you sure are "chic"
From your head to the tip o' your toes,
And if you like us, you just plain like us,
And you don't give a damn who knows.

And Mademoiselle those eyes, Oo la la!
So sparkling, dark and rare,
With the love of all the ages lying
Deep and dormant there.

(Please, please don't think us fickle
That we didn't play the game
But you seemed so human and made to be loved,
And we murmured, "Je vous aime.")

We hear you're going back with us

To the tune of ten thousand wives,
And we wish you ten thousand blessings,
And ten thousand happy lives.

So here's a health to you, Mademoiselle,
Who helped us see it through,
And the load that your laughter lightened
Is the debt that we owe to you.

THE FIRST DIVISION
American Expeditionary Forces, 1917-1919.

When the clarion call of Country
Bade strong men rise and go,
Came they the first of the willing first,
In the pride that leal men know.

When the Eagle soared and its broad wings spread
'Bove the shores of an angered land,
Sailed they the first of the Viking first
Where the treacherous waters spanned.

When the Eagle's Brood awoke to the shriek
Of the great shells day and night,
First of the flock bled they beneath
The star-flare's blinding light.

When the lunging, torn front lines locked
And the strife raged man and man,
Swept they the first of the fighting first
And the van of the battle van.

From the training days of Gondrecourt
Demange—cold, wet and gray
To the trenches north of Lunéville
To Bouconville—Xivray—

To the crater-pitted, wasted tracts
Of war-torn Picardy,
And the ghastly rubble hilltop
Where Cantigny used to be:

To the splendid days of Soissons
The crisis of the strife:
To where giant pincers severed
St. Mihiel as a knife:

To the glorious, stubborn struggle
Up the rugged Argonne slopes,
Till the gates of Sedan crumbled

With the Vandals' crumbling hopes.

Sweeping in conquering columns
To the banks of the vaunted Rhine
Ever the first of the fighting first,
And the Lords of the Battle Line.

LITTLE GOLD CHEVRONS ON MY CUFFS

Little gold chevrons on my cuffs,
What do you mean to me?
"We to the left mean hike and drill,
Trenches and mud and heat and chill
And I to the right for the blood ye spill
Where the Marne runs to the sea."

Little gold chevrons on my cuffs,
What is the tale ye tell?
"We to the left, of the long months spent
Where the somber seasons slowly blent
And I to the right, of the ragged rent
That took so long to get well."

Little gold chevrons on my cuffs,
What do you say to me?
"That ye would not trade us, master mine,
For ribbon or cross or rank, in fine,
That you are ours and we are thine
Through all the years to be."

A TRIP-WIRE

If you're sneaking around on a night patrol,
Trying to miss each cock-eyed hole,
And you choke back a curse from the depths of your soul
It's a trip-wire.

If you think there isn't a thing around
Except the desolate, shell-torn ground,
And you stumble and roll like a spool unwound
It's a trip-wire.

If you know a murmur would give the alarm,
And you've smothered a cough in the crotch of your arm,
And then you go falling all over the farm
It's a trip-wire.

If it's cold and it's rainy and everything's mud,
And you're groping your way through a nice little flood,
And you stand on your head with an elegant thud
It's a trip-wire.

When silence is golden (for "news" is the quest),
And you're returning and stepping your best,
And your rifle goes part way and you go the rest
It's a trip-wire.

THE FAVORITE SONG
("There's a long, long Trail.")

They sing a song that the pines of Maine
Hear in the winter's blast
They sing a song that the riders hum,
Where the cattle plains spread vast;
But there is one they love the most
And they keep it for the last.

They sing the lays of Puget Sound
Aglimmering in the sun—
Of the cotton fields of Alabam',
Where the Gulf-bound rivers run,
But one they sing with a wistful look,
When all the rest are done.

They chant of the land of Dixie,
And their "Little Gray Home in the West"
Of how they'll "can the Kaiser"
And they roar with bellowing zest;
But one they sing as it were a prayer
The song they love the best.

From Xivray to Cantigny
From Soissons to the Meuse
From the Argonne wilds to the white-clad Vosges
Agleam in the dawn's first hues
They sing a sacred song, for it
Is red with battle-dews.

For it is sanctified by space
And the cruel wheel of Time;
And sacrifice has hallowed it,
And mellowed every rhyme,
Until it wells from weary throats
A thing men call sublime.

In frozen trench and billet
In mire, muck and rain
Where the roar of unleashed batteries
Hurl forth their fires again;
At rest, or back in Blighty,
Torn with shell and pain

There's a song they dub the fairest
There's a lilt they love the best
"There's a long, long trail awinding"
To the haven of their quest,
Where the tip of the rainbow reaches
A land in the golden west.

CAPTAIN BLANKBURG
"When Greek meets Greek."
I
They knew he was a German
They thought he was a spy
Toujours they "covered" him and said,
"We'll catch him by-and-by."

They tried to find, by word or act,
In front-line trench or rear,
Some circumstance that would betray
His treacherous dealings clear.

They scanned his face when hostile flares
Set No Man's Land alight
They watched him when the Hun barrage
Tore craters left and right.

They noted every move he made,
With ever wakeful eye,
Reiterating o'er and o'er,
"We'll catch him by-and-by."

II
At last the opportunity
Loomed large in fact and view,
And every near-sleuth in the bunch
Saw that his hunch was true.

Because, upon an inky night,
When mist hung o'er the nation,
The captain took a picked patrol
To gather information.

And as they crept on hands and knees,
In Land No Man may own,
Their stomachs struck the dew-wet grass
With never sound or moan.

(The reason being that the Boche,
On selfsame errand set,
Were creeping hitherward unseen

And likewise mad and wet.)

'Twas then the detail turned their heads
To where their captain lay,
And every rifle in that squad
Was pointed straight his way.

And he? He running true to form,
Two inches raised his chin,
And spouted German volubly
In accents clear and thin.

Click, click, click, click, click, down the line
Each safety-catch turned o'er,
But the captain did not hesitate,
And merely talked the more.

In conversation friendly
He rambled gently on
Unto the Boches' leader,
Till it was nearly dawn.

The while his men they "covered" him
The while their hearts grew black
And you could feel the trigger fingers
Squeezing up the slack.

Just what the purport of his last
Remark was, no one knew,
But in a burst of confidence
A Boche head rose in view. . . .

Across the four-fold stillness
That covers No Man's Land,
An automatic pistol shot
Rang clear and piercing and

The next day German papers told
How Captain Skunk von Skee
Was killed by a Yankee captain,
And Yankee treachery.

LITTLE WAR MOTHERS
When you look at his picture and your eyes
Are dimmed and mighty wet,
And it seems as though your trembling hands
Could reach and touch him yet:
When you faintly call and he answers not
Your supplicating prayer,
Remember his last thought was You:

I know—for I was there.

When the day is done and the hearth-fire glows,
And you slowly knit and knit;
And your furtive eyes from the embers rise
To where he used to sit:
And you feel he never can slip up
And kiss you unaware,
Remember his last word was You:
I know—for I was there.

When your dear brave heart is breaking
And life is 'reft of joy;
And only the spark of memory
The face of a boy—your boy:
May the good God hover over you,
And touch your silvered hair,
And tell you what I've tried to tell:
He knows — for He was there.

INTERRUPTED CHOW

I've had some mighty narrow calls
Some close shaves not a few,
But one of the fairly closest
I'll now narrate to you.

'Twas midnight—hush! the plot grows thick
Crowd close, and hold your breath
'Twas midnight—and the slum-cart came
Upon its round of death.

(It isn't really that the slum
Was quite as bad as that,
But the playful Boche so often dropped
A shell where it was at.)

'Twas midnight—and our appetites
Were whetted large and keen,
As trench feed, once a day, must leave
An interval between.

And so we sought the buzzy-cart,
"Mess-kits alert" and found
It standing in a quiet spot
Where never came a sound

Excepting that of bursting shells
Across the field a way,
(But as I said before, the Boche
Is very given to play).

All innocent and hungry-like
And empty to the core,
I came upon that buzzy-cart,
With never thought of war.

More calm, beneficent and mild
More free from things of strife
I promise you I never was
In all my mortal life.

The air was fair, the stars were out,
The mocking-bird sang clear;
The poppies bloomed, the sergeants fumed,
And food was very near.

When suddenly the ground gave way
It seemed a mile or more
And the whole adjacent landscape leapt
To heaven with a soar.

Earth, rocks and stars commingling
In a swirling mass arose,
Where I, recumbent in the hole,
Assumed an easy pose.

And when I found that I was there
Both arms, both legs, and head,
I picked me up and cogitated
Why I wasn't dead.

For information looked I 'round
North, south and east and west
But the good platoon had up and cleared
Some several feet with zest.

(And the strangest phase of the whole strange thing,
For me to understand,
Was that when I got up I had
My mess-kit in my hand.)

And there I stood and gazed me down
Upon the hole and mud,
And found I was alive because
That blamed shell was a "dud."

A dud's a shell that fails to burst
Whose crater's microscopic
And as I'd just sunk down in it,
My Fates were philanthropic

For had the bally thing gone off
Instead of sitting jake
You'd ne'er have found my scattered parts
With a hair-comb or a rake.

You'd ne'er have found your humble slave
For, sprinkled east and west,
My sad remains would scarce have bulged
The pocket of your vest.

A finger in Benares
A toe in Timbuctoo
And on the Mountains of the Moon
A portion of my shoe.

An eye on Kinchinjanga
To greet the snow-peaked morn;
An ear at Cape Lopatka,
And my dog-tag at the Horn.

S. O. S.
(Service of Supply.)

There's an S. O. S. behind the Lines
That feeds us shells and hardtack,
And guns and clothes and beans and things,
And heals our wounds and pain.
There's an S. O. S. across the seas
That knits for us and writes to us,
Buys bonds and whoops it up for us,
And cheers us on again.

There's an S. O. S. behind the Lines,
We could not do without it:
Just go and ask the Army,
If you'd know the reasons why.
There's an S. O. S. across the seas,
And if you ever doubt it,
Just go and ask a soldier,
Who will promptly black your eye.

THE GAS-PROOF MULE
I've heard the cat hath nine lives,
The hen and worm I've seen,
But a genuine, long eared, gas-proof mule
Is the toughest thing they wean.

Each night he hauled the water-cart
(And to know what Water means,

You have to see a trench-bound bunch
When filling their canteens).

However, no digression now,
But straightway to my story,
And I'll paint that black mule white
And crowned with a crown of glory.

We crowded 'round the faucets
On each, six waited turns
The thirstiest crew I ever knew
With the ingrowing thirst that burns.

And all was peace and quiet
The pause before the storm
When the distant, whirling, demon shriek
Of the G. I. Cans took form.

And when the third one got our range,
With haste, but dignity,
We sought the dugouts 'cross the road,
Calm, though precipitously.

But the fastest thing I've seen on legs,
And I've seen the best, at that.
Was the water-mule when he took the road
At a hundred in nothing flat.

Whether he headed for gay Paree
For Brussels or Berlin
We didn't stop to figure out
But he sure was headed in.

We only thought of our thirst next day,
And a song we'd heard afar,
Of the farm recruit who bade good-bye
To his "mule with the old hee-haw."

Well, all that night they threw us gas
And high explosive shells,
And four long hours we wore our masks,
To ward the murderous smells.

And when the first white streak of dawn
Told "Stand-to" was begun,
We stumbled back and took our posts
To wait our friend the Hun.

The Hun did not appear, but gas
Thick clothed both hill and dale
In clouds and sheets of dead-man's drab,

And down in the deepest vale

With perfect poise and nonchalance,
Sang-froid and savoir-faire,
Browsed that fool mule, capaciously,
With never thought or care.

INFANTRY OF THE WORLD WAR
They shall tell of the Arms resplendent
The men who dared the air;
They shall tell of the work of the mighty guns
Where the far horizons flare:
They shall tell the tale of the Centaurs
Each rear and flanking drive
And the song of the Service of Supply,
That kept them all alive.

And when they seem to have finished,
And ye think that the chant is done,
They will tell the tale of the tramping men
In the sweat of a torrid sun.
They will tell the tale of the marching men
Who plod the live-long night,
To reach the crest at the break o' dawn
When the Nations go to fight.

They will tell the tale of the tired men
Beneath a straining load;
Mile by mile with lunging step
And glassy stare on the road.
They will tell the tale of the front-line trench,
And the one cold meal at night,
And the terrible song of the bursting shells,
And the flares' uncanny light.

They will tell the tale of the moving ranks
When the zero hour lifts,
And the khaki lines leap forward
In the face of the steel-shod drifts.
Where the great shots split asunder,
And clutter hill and plain
With the weary bodies of the men
Who may not march again.

And so for a wide World's wonder,
And the ages yet to be,
They will sing in deathless numbers
The song of the Infantry.
They will slowly close the volume
The story fully told, And a tear shall fall on the cover,

Whose letters are flaming gold.

THE FLOWERS OF FRANCE
The flowers of France are blooming
Upon this bright June day,
The flowers of France are fragrant
And smiling swing and sway,
(For what is death and carnage
A dozen miles away?)

The flowers of France are blooming
Among the wheat and grass
The scarlet headed poppies
That nod you as you pass,
And the blue cornflowers' brilliant hue,
And the daisies in a mass.

The flowers of France are blooming
And beckoning in the breeze,
And laughing in the sunshine,
And bending to the bees,
(But the wooden crosses in a row
Oh what know they of these?)

The flowers of France are blooming
In every rainbow shade,
And as a rainbow is an arch
By tears of heaven made,
I wonder if the flowers of France
Are the tears that France has paid?

A FIRST-CLASS PRIVATE
I haven't a worry or a care
My mind's "at ease" and furled:
For I'm a First-class Private,
And I'm Sitting on the World.

The Loot, before the whole platoon,
He up and called me forth
To drill my squad, "Squads east" and "west,"
Not mentioning south and north.
To drill my squad, "Squads 'round-about,"
For all the World to see
But I'm a First-class Private and
That's good enough for me.

The Loot he is a dandy man
And all that kind of thing,
And I know he wants to see how I

A corporal's job could swing:
But back here in a "rest town"
It just means dirty work,
And I must take the bawling-out
For what the squad may shirk.

'Tis I they'd turn and eye with scorn
If some gun wasn't clean;
'Tis I would play the wet nurse
For a rookie none could wean:
And if a pair of frozen shoes
Makes Smith miss reveille,
It isn't Smith or "Sunny France,"
It's me, yes dammit, me.

So forth I take the Squad to drill,
With ne'er a fault or slip;
But a smile is in my glance, forsooth,
And a jest is on my lip,
Akidding with each friend o'mine
And the Loot was never fain
To try to make a non-com
Of Private Me again.

Oh nothing, oh no nothing
May your resolution shake,
When you're a First-class Private,
And you know you're Sitting Jake.

BIRDS OF BATTLE

Keats sings in peerless stanzas
To the lovely Nightingale
And Shelley tells of the Skylark
Above the summer gale
But I to the Birds of Battle
Needs lift my numbers frail.

For far by the out-flung wires,
Where the shell-torn tree stumps stand,
And over the barren, hole-strewn tracks
Of the wastes of No Man's Land,
In the morning light and the black of night,
The Birds of Battle stand.

No shrieking shots may quell them
Nor gloom nor storm nor rain,
As out of the crash or stillness
A wondrous, shrill refrain
Cuts clear and glad and lithesome
Above the death-strewn plain.

The weary heavens welcome,
And echo back the song,
And weary soldiers linger,
And pause to listen long
To the one glad cry in a war-torn sky,
That holds so much of wrong.

ONLY FOR YOU.

The torturous hike up the hill road,
Plowing through snow and mud;
The poor weary arches breaking
The socks that are wet with our blood:
The terrible, binding, burning strap
That's cutting our shoulder through
And our parched lips stammer, "My Country,
For you and only for you."

The slight and the slur and the nagging
We must take from a rowdy or cad;
And we simply salute and say "Yes sir,"
And pretend that we never feel mad:
Though our heart is a forest of hatred
And justice seems hidden from view
And we mutter, "For you, oh my Country
For you, yea, and only for you."

When all evening long the guns' reddened glares
Turn night into hellish day,
Till in Berserker rage their silver bursts cut
The drab of the dawn's growing gray:
When over the top we are starting again
Full knowing the thing that we do
We murmur, "For you, oh my Country
For you, aye and only for you."

COOTIES.

Some people call 'em Totos
Some people call 'em Lice;
Some people call 'em several things
That really aren't nice;
But the Soldier calls 'em "Cooties,"
So "Cooties" must suffice.

We've met the dear Mosquito
We've met the festive Fly
It seems to me we've seen the Flea
That jumpeth far and high;
Yea, we have known various bugs

Though not the reason why.

But when you're in the trenches
And cannot take a bath,
As one canteen of water
Is all one day one hath,
You raise the comely Cooties
Who raise, in turn, your wrath.

You can't escape the Cooties
By day nor yet by night.
No G. I. Can alarms them,
Nor other sound of fight.
Not even Gas affects them
Which doesn't seem just right.

You may not eat, you may not sleep,
You may not bat an eye:
You may not duck a six-inch shell
That's singing gaily by,
But that a Cootie, like the Poor,
Is with you—very nigh.

They bite you singly and in squads,
They have a whole parade;
They form a skirmish line and sweep
Across each hill and glade;
But seek their dugouts when you think
Your grip is firmly laid.

It does no good to curse 'em
They cannot hear or talk.
It does no good to chase 'em
To still-hunt or to stalk.
The only thing is hand-grenades,
At which, 'tis said, they balk.

Oh Cooties, little Cooties,
You have no sense of shame;
You are not fair, you are not square,
You do not play the game
But east and west and south and north
Is spread afar your fame.

OLD FUSEE
(Rifle number 366915, Springfield model 1903.)

I really hate to leave you,
Old Fusee
Where the land is scarred and peeled,

And the broken battlefield
Bears its red and deadly yield
Wearily.

I really hate to leave you,
Old Fusee
To the wind and dew and rain
Of a shorn and shotted plain,
Till stranger hands again
Discover thee.

I really hate to leave you,
Old Fusee
To the clinging, clogging dust
To the all-destroying crust
Of a clawing, gnawing rust
Unmercifully.

I really hate to leave you,
Old Fusee
But they've plugged me good and hard,
So I quit you, trusty pard,
As I creep back rather marred,
To old Blightee.

I really hate to leave you,
Old Fusee
With your bore a brilliant sheen,
And your metals black and clean,
Where your brown striped stock and lean
Gleams tigerishly.

I really hate to leave you,
Old Fusee
For the wanton weather's hate,
And careless hands to desecrate
Barrel, bolt and butt and plate,
Unthinkingly.

I really hate to leave you,
Old Fusee
And I bear a double pain
As I pause to turn again
Where I left you on the plain,
Unwillingly.

THE COLORS OF BLIGHTY

The shades of red an' white an' blue
Mean rather more to me an' you,
Than just parades an' bands an' such

And hollerin' loud an' talking much.

The wounds are dark and red
All jagged-red in Blighty:
And untamed hearts are red
Where, stretching bed on bed,
Lies lax each weary head,
In Blighty.

The walls are blank and white
All fresh and white in Blighty:
And cheeks are gaunt and white,
Where through the endless night
They fight the second fight,
In Blighty.

Outside the skies are blue
Soft, cloud-flecked blue o'er Blighty
But clear, relentless blue
Of purpose steeled anew
Lies there revealed to you
In every eye in Blighty.

The shades of red an' white an' blue
Mean rather more to me an' you,
Than just parades an' bands an' such
And hollerin' loud an' talking much.

WHEN NURSE COMES IN
(Convalescent stage.)

The stories sure are rich and rare,
They'd strike you blind, they'd turn your hair,
They're dark as coal down in the bin
Till Nurse comes in.

The language is an awful hue,
Astreak with crimson shades and blue;
'Twould scorch a mammoth's leather skin
Till Nurse comes in.

Words run the gamut of the trench
They beat old Mustard Gas for stench,
They rise with oscillating din
Till Nurse comes in.

The cussin's quaint and loud and strong,
Imported stuff, that don't belong
In dictionaries fat or thin
Till Nurse comes in.

And then you'd be surprised to hear
The change of pace, the shift o' gear,
The dainty tales that just begin
When Nurse comes in.

CHARLIE CHAPLIN IN BLIGHTY

The mess-hall windows blanketed
To bar the western light
The tables cleaned and cleared away,
And bench by bench in close array
Five hundred convalescents sway
To catch the caption bright.

And there are men with helpless legs,
And torn chest and back;
And men with arms in sling and splint,
And one poor eye that bears no glint,
And muscles limp or turned to flint
And souls upon the rack.

They came from Chateau Thierry
From Fere-en-Tardenois
From Soissons, Oulchy-le-Chateau,
From Rheims and Fismes, where blow by blow,
'Cross Marne and Oureq and Vesle aflow
They hammered them afar.

And now upon the screen is thrown
An old familiar form:
'Tis Charlie of the strong appeal,
At skating-rink or riot meal,
And every mirth-producing reel
Awakes the farthest dorm.

The aching head, the splintered arm,
The weary, dragging feet;
The wound that took a month to drain
The everlasting, gnawing pain
Are all forgot and gone again
When Charlie strikes the street.

Your esoteric shrug and sneer
And call him crude and quaint;
But we who've seen him "over here"
Who've heard the laugh that brings the tear
Who've heard the bellowing roar and cheer
We call him Charles the Saint.

TWO WORLDS

Here in the Jardin des Plantes of Nantes
I sit in the nickering shade,
Watching the scampering children play
And the way of a man and a maid
And the noble women of France in the black
Of a Nation unafraid.

The lace of the shadows across the paths
Where the warm sun niters through,
And the open vista between the trees,
With the swan pond half in view,
And the flowers and sloping lawns and the pines
'Neath an arch of Brittany's blue.

The air is soft as a day in June,
The blossoms manifold
Throw streaks and patches of rainbow hue
Across the green and gold,
And earth and sky in witchery
Entwine you in their hold.

And it comes to me, Can it really be
But two full moons have fled,
Since I limped from a scarred and riven field
Where lay the newly dead,
Bathed in the light of a splendid fight,
And blotched with their blood's own red.

A world of crimson slaughter
Where the grim locked legions sway
And the mad machine guns whistle
Their endless roundelay
And the sinister sound of the thundering pound
Of the great guns night and day.

Night and day, night and day,
With scarce a pause between,
As out of the empty dark a voice
From the farthest hills unseen,
Comes whirling, swirling, shrieking down
Where the helpless front lines lean.

The air is soft as a morn in June
The filmy shadows sway;
And only the joyous music
Of the prattle of children at play,
And the gentle rustle of whispering leaves
That tell of the closing day.

EMBARKATION HOME

If you're a homebound soldier
Who's done his little best,
And you are going 'board the boat
At St. Nazaire or Brest,
Bordeaux or any other port,
Steam-up and headed west:

If you are full o' the joy o' life
And "pep" and all that stuff;
And the ozone permeates your soul
And makes you gay and bluff,
Don't turn and yell, "Who won the War?
The M Ps,"—Can that guff.

For the M Ps are a sacred caste
That boss the city street
A hundred miles behind the Lines
Where dangers never greet,
Nor roaming shells come swirling by,
Nor surging first waves meet.

So if the long, tense session
Of soul-engulfing war,
And "Prussian" discipline and rule,
And heart-enslaving law
Say, "Open wide the throttle
Of lung and throat and jaw"

Repress that natural impulse,
For you're not human—yet:
Sedately up the gangplank walk,
Eyes front and lips tight set,
Or you'll come back and spend six weeks
In a mud-dump, nice and wet.

The wind is blowing 'cross the bow,
The first smoke lags alee
The sun that's broken through the clouds
Is dancing on the sea,
So, homebound soldier, watch your step,
And take advice from me.

THE STATUE OF LIBERTY

Sing of the Venus de Milo,
The lady without any arms;
Sing of the Venus of this and of that,
And tell of their marvelous charms:
Rave of your wonderful statues,
In divers lands here o'er the sea,

In bushels and reams, but the Girl of our Dreams
Is our godmother, Miss Liberty.

Its contour may not be perfection
Its technique we really don't know
If you ever asked, "Who was the artist?"
It would come as a terrible blow.
But to us it is home, friends and Country,
To us it means all that is best,
'Tis the first that lifts out of the waters
Of "Our little Gray Home in the West."

'Tis the first on that endless horizon
Where the clouds meet the wind driven spume,
And the scavenger gulls wing to greet us
From out of the gathering gloom
'Tis the first that calls beckoning to us
Through the mist of the swaggering sea
"Oh lay down your guns my knight-errant sons,
And come back to the bosom of me."

PART II. PRE-WAR POEMS

TO FRANCE—1917

The sea that kisses France's shore,
It beats on yours and mine.
Her love and faith and chivalry,
That sparkle as her wine,
With all our faith and all our love
Commingling combine.

The colors of the flag of France
Are ours by hue and hue:
The blazing red of courage
The white of purpose true,
And constancy and loyalty
Awoven in the blue.

The spirit and the soul of France,
That shatter fetters free,
They came to us in darkest days
To weld our destiny;
And so with sword in hand we come
To pay our debt to Thee.

To pay our debt a hundredfold
Friend of our new-born years.
To march with you and fight with you,
Till rise the final cheers
And hand in hand, o'er a grave-strewn land,

We blend our mingled tears.

Where blends our blood as once it did
In days of a long gone
When the Bourbon lilies leapt and gleamed
Among the Stars on high
And the white and crimson bands of dawn
Rose in the eastern sky.

And the the white and crimson bands of dawn,
And the Stars that glow and glance,
Shall girdle them their armor on,
With buckler, sword, and lance,
And leap to the charge and sweep the field
With the Trois Couleurs of France,

If right is might and Honor lives
Oh Sister? 'cross the seas
And Liberty and Justice still
Hold high commune with these;
A four-fold vengeans waits the Hun,
And his iniquities.

THE PACIFIST

Cowards and curs and traitors,
Fatuous dreaming fools
Binding us, stripped, for the madman
Nurtured of dastard schools,
Where right of might and who springs first
Are the only known rules.

Well fed, well housed and sleek and smug,
Full pursed and full of pride
Your fields are green, your lanes are fair
Where peaceful homes abide,
And your children play by sunny streams
That laughing seaward glide.

What Primal Power tells you eat
To the ends of your belly-greed
What holds your fields with harvests full,
And answers every need
And bids your bairns play laughingly
With never care or heed?

The answer, Fool, is written large
In words of blazing light
They are rewards of dwelling in
A Land of kingly might,
That grants you surety and wealth

And guards you, day and night.

And whence, Fool, came its splendid strength
And why, and how and when?
In a World of strife and reddened knife
Did it rise by tongue and pen?
No, Dolt, but by the strong right arms,
The arms of its fighting men.

And Ye, Ye would sit with folded hands,
Agaze into Heaven's blue,
With sanctimonious murmurings
Of what the Lord will do;
While your neighbor and your neighbor's son
Go forth and fight for you.

For you, you cur, and your belly-need
For your hearth and kith and kin:
For your harvest and your banking-house
Where you shovel the shekels in,
Till the labor has hardened your hands and heart,
And your soul is parchment skin.

Religion cannot cover
A dog whose liver is white.
Your Christ, with righteous anger,
Smote hard to left and right
The usurers. And never said
He was too proud to fight.

When we are another Belgium
And the land with blood is dyed,
And your homes are burned and your women raped,
And ye know that ye have lied
Mayhap ye will say with your final gasp
That ye are satisfied.

BATTLE HYMN OF 17
On the entry, in 1917, of the United States into the World War.

Not with vain boasts and mouthings
Not with jesting light
But for Duty and Love of Country
Come we in armor dight.

Not for our own advantage
Not for Adventure's lust
Not for the hope of honor
But a Cause that is high and just.

Not for the praise of our fellow-man,
Or greed or gain or creed,
But for the sight of the suffering eyes
That call us in their need.

(The withering, mad machine-guns
Shall drop us one by one,
Where the red, red streams of No Man's Land
Gleam 'neath a blood-red sun.)

(The shriek of the spraying shrapnel
The roar and the blinding glare,
And the gaping crater's dripping fangs
Shall ope and find us there.)

Not in the strong man's tyranny
Or the pride of worldly things,
But guarding clean traditions,
Unstained by the hands of kings.

Not with sudden yearning,
But knowing the risks we dare,
We board the waiting galleons
For a Nation brave and fair.

(For a Nation bearing the battle's brunt
The strength of the Vandals' blast
With an even keel and a steady wheel,
And her Colors nailed to the mast.)

Not with hectic fire,
But weighing the thing we do,
We cross to the coasts of the fighting hosts
To the France our Fathers knew.

Brothers in blood of old—and now
Together to hunt and slay,
Till we drive the Beast to his bone-strewn lair
An eye for an eye—a hair for a hair
And we leave him broken and bleeding there
Forever and a day.

Not with vain boasts and mouthings
But in silent, grim parade
We come, Lord God of Battles,
To the last and great Crusade.

MY SAPPHIRE

I have a sapphire rich and fair
And soft as a velvet sky,
When only the stars are shining low
And the heavens hold a mystic glow
And a hushed world stands agaze to know
The wonderful Whence and Why.

I have a sapphire that I turn
In the dark of somber days:
And the darting tongues of nickering blue
Flash deep and rare in wondrous hue,
Sharp as the lightning, pure as the dew,
And true as m'lady's gaze.

I have a sapphire that I hold
Beneath the chandelier:
And the phosphor of its azure gleam
Sweeps clear as the depths of the mountain stream
Where the Sun-god hurls his molten beam
In the morn of the golden year.

I have a sapphire I adore
Of varying whims and moods
Blue-black it lies with never a mark
Across the dim unfathomed dark,
Till there lifts the glow of a tiny spark
And again it sullen broods.

I have a sapphire that I bend
'Neath the light of burning rays:
And the flames spread forth a fairy fire,
Seething and writhing and leaping higher
Till they come to the land of my heart's desire,
In a glittering, blinding blaze.

I have a sapphire that I hold.
When the goal seems far away:
When the lee shore churns in saffron spume.
And the fluctuant ocean's plume on plume
Bears down to a rock-ribbed hidden doom,
And the sky is ashen gray.

I have a sapphire that I turn;
And the clouds break, and the wine
Of a glorious sun spreads east and west
To where the Islands of the Blest
Raise verdant shores at my behest,
And a golden world is mine.

Oh Sapphire from a distant vale

Where the white Himalayas tower:
Where the Kashmir lakes are royal blue,
And passions strong and hearts are true,
All these are met and blent in you,
A princely heir and dower.

THE TWINS

Out of the wonderful nowhere,
Into the lowly here;
Laughing and loving and lithesome,
And radiating cheer.

Twin rose-buds o' Killarney hue
Fragrant and fresh and fair
And eyes of blue, wide-gazed and true,
And tawny yellow hair.

And smiles as sweet as any meet
In pleasant paths above:
And golden laughter that echoes after,
To finger the chords of love.

Two wee buds o' Killarney hue
That beckon and beguile
And 'neath your spell we're learning well
There is something still worthwhile.

Though drab days break and drab thoughts wake
O'er fields of sleet and snow,
There's sunshine rare just everywhere
For you have taught us so.

ON SENDING MY BOOK TO AN ENGLISH FRIEND

"It's a long lane that knows no turnings"
And the seas are wide indeed,
But there are no barriers dividing
The Anglo-Saxon creed.
Fair fighting when the skies are lowering
Fair peace when skies are clear
And the faith of fair intentions, unfaltering,
And the heart that holds no fear.

"It's a long lane that knows no turnings"
And Browning never said a thing more true,
So I know you'll know the spirit that impels me
To send this little messenger to you.

IMMORTAL KEATS

Matchless bard of all the ages
Lyric sounder of the lyre
Wake among your golden echoes
Rise amid your latent fire
Tell us, Master of the Muses
Sweetest singer ever sung
By what law of Earth or Heaven
Ye were called away so young?

By what law of God or Mammon
By what creed of land or sea
Was a weary World forsaken
Of the mind that harbored thee?
Ere that wondrous mind's fruition
Scarce had grown to the tree.

If the half-fledged sapling gave us
Melodies past human praise
If such virgin buddings crowded
Those few sad and glorious days;
If such flowers, barely opened,
Swept us in a wild amaze

What, Oh Lord and Prince of Poesy,
Would your soul have given to men
What the marvelous meed and measure
Of your pulsing, choral pen
Had your numbered days been lengthened
To a three score years and ten?

As through mystic lands ye led us
O'er the paths your feet had gone:
Pipes of Pan—and fain we followed
Glad and willing slave and pawn,
Till we reached the fields Elysian
Till we faced the gorgeous dawn:

Till the lanes seemed filled with roses
Roses lipped with opal dew:
Till the vales seemed filled with incense
Incense slowly drifting through:
Till the seas seemed filled with grottoes
Grottoes amber, gold and blue:

Till the songs of birds rang clearer
And the sunshine shone more rare,
And the moon above the meadows
Gathered love, and left it there;
And the swaying stars rose whiter
And the World was very fair:

As your thoughts' eternal fountains,
Shot with iridescent gleams,
Floating down through glades enchanted,
On the breast of faery streams,
To a pearl-strewn bay of beryl
Reached the haven of our dreams.

TO A LITTLE GIRL

Flammarion and Kelvin and Herschel every one,
Said Heaven was a hundred, million, billion miles away.
So I couldn't contradict them—it wouldn't do at all
But they had never heard your laughter innocent and gay.

Flammarion and Kelvin and Herschel every one,
They said the Milky Way was fair beyond all human ken:
But they had never seen your face, upturned, aquestioning
A dainty bit of rapture in a leaden world o' men.

Flammarion and Kelvin and Herschel every one,
They told of gorgeous comets and their manes so bright and rare:
But comet glow could never show the living threads of light
That dance and gleam in th' rippling stream and fragrance of
your hair.

Flammarion and Kelvin and Herschel every one,
They said the azure ether stretched in miles of lapis hue;
But they had never known eyes that gaze into your soul
In longing little wonder wells of limpid gray and blue.

Flammarion and Kelvin and Herschel every one,
They said no melody could match the singing of the spheres:
But they had never heard your voice ring joyously at play
The music of a weary world of roil and toil and tears.

Flammarion and Kelvin and Herschel every one.
They've told the tale of the double stars, and their faith the
eons through—
But constant though they be, their hearts could never know the love,
The yearning burning tender love, dear child, we bear for you.

GOD

I
They would give hands to Thee, head to Thee, feet to Thee
They who are blind:
They would give form to Thee, fashion Thee manikin,
After their kind.

They would give hate to Thee, spite to Thee, jealousy
Thou the adored:

Only have fear in Thee, only repel Thee,
Master and Lord.

They would bring shame to Thee, even in worship
Each empty rite:
Bigotry, canting and sere superstition,
Knowing no light.

Faiths esoteric, pedantic and recondite
Mystical creeds:
False and insipid and brutal and selfish
And wrought to their needs.

They whom Ye nurtured from primal conceiving,
And ne'er a flaw
They know Thee not, or in knowing, reject Thee,
Thee and Thy law.

Saying, "We see Thee not, come to us, speak to us
Tangible stand.
Come in the purple, crowned, robed and resplendent
Sceptre in hand.

"Even as kings have done, through all the ages,
Brave to behold
Fanfare of trumpets, be jeweled and refulgent
And girdled with gold:

"Or in a chariot welded of star-dust
Glittering white
Pause at the cloud-line 'mid crashing of thunder
And blazing of light.

"Rolling Thy voice till the Pleiades tremble
The spheres are amoan;
The Earth for a footstool—the outermost planets
Grouped for a throne.

"Thus would we see Thee, acclaim Thee; and worship Thee,
Thou in Thy might
Concrete, conglomerate, human and splendid
Aflame in our sight."

II
They who have drunk of the River of Knowledge
Only a quaff,
Pity them, Father that know not Thy meaning,
Children who laugh.

Atoms that reck not the wherefore of atoms
Dust of the dust:

Groping in darkness, recusant and doubting
And bearing no trust.

They would make mock of Thee, saying the life-spark,
Came not of Thee:
Function by function in wonderful unison
Each mystery.

Sunshine and rain-fall and food to their needing,
Air, sea and land:
Seed-time and fruit-time and harvest and gleaning
Made to their hand.

They would gainsay Thee by calling it Nature,
Calling it Chance:
And by their impotent wonder, Thy glory,
Only enhance.

But when in mercy the last word is spoken
When the gates yawn;
Father of Nations—take Thou Thy children
Into the dawn.

Crowning Thy marvelous works with a crowning
Ultimate—vast
Showing compassion and loving they knew not,
E'en to the last.

THE GOLDEN DAY
Have ye a day that bears the glare
Of the flaming morning sun?
Have ye a day the mind may search,
Weighing what ye have done?

Have ye a day ye are satisfied
Will stand the acid test
From the first gray strand of the eastern skies
To the last red glow in the west?

Have ye a day ye grappled with
And hurled in mortal throes,
When, 'bove the white horizon,
The Great Occasion rose?

Mayhap the World bore witness
To the things of your Golden Day:
Mayhap it is locked from the gaze of men,
And ye've thrown the key away.

NOTES & GLOSSARY

Trenches

French Lorraine - Lorraine is now French, but, of course, it was not so during the war.

Kultur - The so-called German culture.

Barb-Wire Posts

Herein is described a common optical illusion or phenomenon seen by all soldiers, old and young, experienced or green, during the long night vigils looking through the wires, across No Man's Land.

Boche - A German.

Hun - A German. The people of Germany take great exception to being called "Huns," protesting that they are not of this stock. After the defeat of Attila and his Huns at Chalons, in 451 A. D., by the combined efforts of the Celts themselves, the indigenous people of France, the Romans, who were still masters of the country, the Franks, who had already become a power in the land, having advanced as far south as the Somme, and the Visigoths, who, early in the same century, had established their great empire in southern France and Spain; after this great battle the Huns retreated back into Germany, where many of their descendants must still be, but of course the majority of the German people are not, from an ethnological standpoint, Huns. The reason for this appelation being applied to them is simply that when a people have the attributes of a Hun, they must expect to be so designated. A man may very properly be called a pig without any misapprehension that he actually travels upon four hoofs. However, it is possible, though not probable, that the leopard may change his spots; and time, and contact with civilization, and a democratic form of government may eventually eradicate the present very marked idiosyncrasies of the German race.

Your Gas-Mask

"full-field" - The full-field pack, consisting of blankets, shelter-half, clothing, extra shoes, etc., weighing over 50 pounds, on the back of an infantryman, and guaranteed to increase 50 pounds in weight every five kilometers after the first ten kilometer mark has been passed.

full marching-order - The full-field pack as described above, plus rifle, cartridge-belt with a hundred rounds of ammunition, two bandoliers, each containing a hundred extra rounds, gas-mask, mess outfit and the steel helmet, commonly known as your tin hat.

Slum and Beef Stew

Josephus - Josephus Daniels, Secretary of the Navy during the war.

Gobs - Nickname for sailors.

Brains of the Army - Any order apparently wrong or ridiculous is generally provocative of the soldiers saying, "Brains of the Army."

Thotmes III, (or Thutmose or Thutmosis) - Of the Eighteenth Dynasty, who began his reign about 1500 B. C., Egypt's greatest conqueror, and under whom the Egyptian Empire attained its largest extent. Rameses II (the Great) of the following Dynasty, is, however, the more generally known.

Cyrus' doughboys swept etc. - Refers to the passage of Cyrus and his great army through the Cilician Gates, on his way from his conquest of Lydia in Asia Minor, to his descent of the Euphrates Valley to Babylon, whose easy capitulation in 539 B. C. finally brought to an end the old glory of the Babylonian Empire, which, after a long period under Assyrian rule, had blossomed forth in a glorious recrudescence, in the latter part of the Seventh Century B. C, under Nebopolassar and his famous son Nebuchadnezzar—and then known as the Neo-Babylonian Empire, or, more commonly, as Chaldea. The reader will doubtless remember that it was through the same passage in the Taurus Mountains that Ashurbanapal, le Grand Monarque of Assyria when at the apogee of her power in the Seventh Century B. C, and also Alexander the Great, sweeping to his eastern conquests, both passed.

Doughboys is the popular present-day nickname for infantrymen.

Sitting on the World - When the situation is thoroughly agreeable and everything is "breaking" just right.

S.O.L. - Well known soldier expression which, elegantly translated, means being totally and entirely out of luck, but not to be adopted for "polite conversation." Remember this admonition.

Mr. Fly
G.I. Cans - Large high-explosive shells of about 6 inches diameter or over, and made of thick galvanized iron or what appeared to be such.

Cooties
Are pleasant little neighbors in the trenches, due to the inadequacy of bathing facilities.

The Salvation Army With the A. E. F.
John Doe. Private Doe - The designation of an American soldier, where no specific name is used, as, for example, to fill in the place for a name on a sample blank or application of any kind. Not used as a popular nickname for the American soldier as Tommy Atkins is used for the British soldier.

A. E. F. - American Expeditionary Forces: the title of the American troops in France during the war.

Shell-Holes
The "77" - The typical artillery piece of the German army, and having a calibre of approximately three inches, roughly corresponding with the famous French "75," though not as effective, but quite effective enough.

Food
Salvation - Salvation Army.

Song of the Volunteers of 1917
Bayard - The great chivalric hero and warrior of France during the reign of Francis I. The Chevalier Bayard was killed in northern Italy in 1524, during the advance of Bourbon at the head of the Imperial forces.

The Cid - The chief heroic figure of Spain, who lived in the Eleventh Century, fighting ably against the Moorish power until exiled by his king in the year 1075, after which he became a free lance, sometimes engaging in battle the Infidel and sometimes the Christian. He died in 1099, and, while a very able commander, it is generally understood that most of his great deeds are a gorgeous fabric of tradition rather than actual history.

Artillery Registering - The bursting of shrapnel over your trenches, by the enemy, in order to get the range for their shell-fire which is to follow.

Trucks
Toto - A nickname for a Cootie, qv.

Including nuts, candy etc. - The American soldier has a notoriously "sweet-tooth," and big husky men positively gormandize on things saccharine, when obtainable.

Mademoiselle - The army man pronounces the word "mademoiselle" at full length, using the most punctilious care to enunciate each and every one of the four syllables. Whether this is due to the word being foreign to many of them, or whether it is due to their all-saving subtle sense of American humor, so that it seems rather delicious to call the little French ladies by so long and ponderous a title, I really do not know, but I strongly suspect that it is the latter.

The First Division - Caesar had his Tenth Legion, Napoleon had his Old Guard, and the American Army during the World War had its First Division. It might therefore not seem entirely malapropos to quote the words of the great French general Mangin, who was the corps commander of the First Division of the American Army, the famous First Moroccans of the French Army and the Second Division of the American Army, at the Second Battle of the Marne, that began on July 18th, 1918, and was the turning point of the whole war. In this great door movement the First Division was given practically the post of honor at the hinge itself, i.e., directly at Soissons, only one division, the 153rd French Infantry Division, being on the inside of the First Division, and as it was in this engagement that a gentleman of Teutonic origin, operating a machine-gun from our extreme left flank, and apparently very much irritated about something, put a bullet in my side and out my back, it is only natural that the message of Gen. Mangin was of interest to me, and saved, and here quoted verbatim:—

Lauds Americans in Battle. - General Mangin Thanks Pershing's Men for Brilliant Part in Drive. (By Associated Press.)

With the French. Army in France, Aug. 7.—General Mangin, who was in direct command of the Allied forces in the drive against the German right flank south of Soissons, has issued the following order of the day thanking the American troops for their brilliant participation in the battle which caused the German retreat between the Marne and the Aisne:

"Officers, non-commissioned officers and soldiers of the Third American Army Corps:

"Shoulder to shoulder with your French comrades, you threw yourselves into the counter-offensive begun on July 18th. You ran to it like going to a feast. Your magnificent dash upset and surprised the enemy and your indomitable tenacity stopped counter-attacks by his fresh divisions. You have shown yourselves to be worthy sons of your great country and have gained the admiration of your brothers in arms.

"Ninety-one cannon, 7,200 prisoners, immense booty and ten kilometers (six and a quarter miles) of reconquered territory are your share of the trophies of this victory. Besides this, you have acquired a feeling of your superiority over the barbarian enemy against whom the children of liberty are fighting. To attack him is to vanquish him.

"American comrades, I am grateful to you for the blood you generously spilled on the soil of my country. I am proud of having commanded you during such splendid days, and to have fought with you for the deliverance of the world."

"The Stars and Stripes," the weekly paper of the A. E. F. in France, in giving a tabulated form of the record of the various divisions, and their insignia, which was worn on the shoulder of the left sleeve, said the following of the First Division:—

Division Insignia: Crimson figure "1" on khaki background, chosen because the numeral "1" represents the number of the division and many of its subsidiary organizations. Also, as proudly claimed, because it was the "First Division in France; first in sector; first to fire a shot at the Germans; first to attack; first to conduct a raid; first to be raided; first to capture prisoners; first to inflict casualties; first to suffer casualties; first to be cited singly in General Orders; first in the number of Division, Corps and Army Commanders and General Staff Officers produced from its personnel."

To this might have been added that the First Division, which was a Regular Army division, and originally comprised about twenty or thirty per cent "old soldiers," and the rest of us "war volunteers," but proud of being "Regulars," the First Division, which consisted of the 16th, 18th, 26th and 28th Infantry Regiments, the 5th, 6th and 7th Field Artillery Regiments, the 1st Engineer Regiment, and a complement of Cavalry, etc., was the division that General Pershing, the commander-in-chief, picked out to fill the most vital positions on important occasions, as, for example, when, from the whole army, he chose the First Division to go into the front line just west of Montdidier, at the Battle of Picardy, to help hold the very apex of the huge German bulge that had swept southwestward from St. Quentin to Montdidier, in the great series of Hun drives which started on March 21st. 1918. Again, it was the First Division that Pershing placed at Soissons at virtually the hinge of the great door movement in the turning point of the whole war, the Second Battle of the Marne, as heretofore described; and it was the First Division to which Pershing again gave the post of honor when the St. Mihiel salient was closed, as it was this Division that was placed on the inside position of the great southern jaw, just east of Xivray and dangerous Mont Sec.

Casualties and kilometers make very interesting reading, but when a Commander-in-chief consistently and persistently picks out one certain division for the most difficult and all-important positions, there is not much room for argumentation.

Mr. Page, in his article in The World's Work, for May. 1919. In describing the Second Battle of the Marne, tells how the First Division went over the top with the 153rd French Infantry Division on its left, and the famous First Moroccan Division and the Second Division of the American Army on its right, and how, in this gruelling engagement, the First Division outlasted both the Second Division and the First Moroccans, and really also the 153rd French Division on its left, as this latter was obliged to get reinforcements, Mr. Page recapitulating the situation with the following paragraph:—

"When the division (the First Division) finally came out of the line it had lost more than 7,200 men, mostly in the infantry. The full complement of infantry in a division is 12.000. Five days' constant and successful attack after a long march: an advance of more than six and a quarter miles (ten kilometers); losses of at least 50 per cent, of the infantry engaged: keeping pace with the famous Moroccan Division and staving longer in the fight—all this had demonstrated that the 1st Division could stand in any company." In mentioning these facts there is no desire on my part to pretend that this outfit single-handed won the war, because, if I said that, I would be talking sheer nonsense. The consensus of opinion both at home and abroad, seems to be that the whole American Army lived entirely up to expectations, so that any man who was in a combat division, has good reason to feel proud of his own division, irrespective of what one that may have been. With this little word of explanation I feel at liberty to quote the following which appeared in the Paris edition of The New York Herald:—

Prowess of Yanks Compels Praise Even from Hun,
(Special telegram to the Herald.)
From Burr Price.
With the American Armies.
Friday

From a captured officer of the German army comes a remarkable tribute to the fighting prowess of the First Division of the American troops, whose work will go down in history as among the most remarkable of the present war.

He declared the Germans did not believe the Americans could produce, within five years, a division such as they had found the First Division to be. The German, when taken, had seen four years of severe fighting. This is what he had to say yesterday:—

"I received orders to hold the ground at all costs. The American barrage advanced toward my position and the work of your artillery was marvelous. The barrage was so dense that it was impossible for us to move out of our dugouts.

"Following the barrage closely were the troops of the First Division. I saw them forge ahead and knew that all was lost. All night I remained in my dugout, hoping vainly that something would happen that would permit me to rejoin my army. This morning your troops found me and here I am, after four years of fighting, a prisoner.

"Yesterday, I knew that the First Division was opposite us, and I knew we would have to put up the hardest fight of the war. The First Division is wonderful and the German army knows it.

"We did not believe that within five years the Americans could develop a division such as this First Division. The work of its infantry and artillery is worthy of the best armies of the world."

Little Gold Chevrons on My Cuffs - The gold chevrons, called "stripes," worn on the cuffs of "overseas" soldiers, during the World War, each one on the left cuff standing for six months' "overseas" service, and each chevron on the right cuff standing for a wound. One wound chevron meant a wound or wounds severe enough to take a man back to the hospital, irrespective of whether he had one or a dozen bullets or pieces of shell in him on that occasion.

Captain Blankburg - The patrol herein described was what was called a "reconnoitring patrol," sent out solely for the purpose of gathering information, keeping itself unknown to the enemy, and not fighting unless actually attacked. "Combat patrols" were sent out for this latter purpose.

Interrupted Chow
Buzzy-cart - The carts that were sent from the company kitchens, which were usually from six to ten kilometers back of the first line trenches, up to within about two to four kilometers of the front line, where they would stop at designated points until chow details from the second line came back to them, to carry the cans of slum, coffee, and the bread or hardtack, up to the men in the first and second line. All this, of course, was done under cover of darkness, but as the Germans had the range

of all the roads, etc., and knew at about what time the food had to be gone after, it meant that almost every night at least one detail was shot to pieces.

Dog-tag - Small, round metal disc, suspended from the neck by a cord, and with the soldier's name, rank and organization stamped thereon, and forming an identification tag.

The Gas-Proof Mule
"Stand-to" - In the first and second line trenches everyone was obliged to remain awake all night, but at dawn each man had to take his exact post, and be prepared to repel any enemy attack that might come over, as that was a favorite hour for doing so. This was called "stand-to."

Infantry of the World War
Zero hour - The exact time at which you start forward to attack.

A First-Class Private
Loot - Abbreviation for lieutenant.

"Sunny France" - Soldier sarcasm, because he scarcely ever saw any sun while in France, and, of course, the majority had never visited the Riviera, nor known Paris in summer raiment, during normal peace times.

Sitting Jake - Means the same thing as "Sitting on the World," i.e., everything salubrious and "breaking" just right.

Note
While realizing that my personal affairs are of no possible interest to the reader, it would seem, however, almost obligatory for me to do myself justice, and explain that I was quite willing to shoulder responsibility, which this poem might make it appear I was not. Hence the following little anecdote:—During a rest period back from the trenches, which was the only occasion when you had time to bother your head about smaller things, several men had applied for officers' commissions, so I got some civilian letters of recommendation, and put in an application to be permitted to go up for examination for a commission. This application was forwarded "approved" by my company commander, together with personal recommendations from my three previous company commanders. As this officer is the one who sees you daily, his recommendation is, from a military standpoint, of more value than that of a major-general. But in spite of my application being forwarded with the approval of all four of the company commanders that I had had up to that time, it was disapproved higher up by someone who very seldom could ever have even seen me. But having had no thought or intention of getting a commission, when I entered the Army, and having crossed over to Europe as a civilian, at my own expense, in August, 1917, to enlist in the American Army in France, which I did on September 1st, 1917, in Paris, so as to absolutely insure getting into the trenches, and as at the time of my application I had already accomplished my purpose, it may readily be discerned that the return of my application did not perturb the habitual equanimity of my soul, nor cause me to lose any of my natural sleep or youthful charm.

Only for You
rowdy or cad - While very often some junior, or even senior, officer would fall under this category, and even worse, the majority of them really tried to give their men a square deal. If an officer were a rough-neck, snob, or as the men in the ranks would usually express it, a ribbon-counter clerk, it was only quite natural that he would take cowardly advantage of his shoulder straps to make it as miserable as possible for the men under him, but if an officer were a gentleman in civilian life, the man in the ranks was sure to be handled as a man and treated fairly, so long as he did his military

duty and conducted himself as a soldier. Of this latter type, I can look back with pleasure on all my company commanders, remembering especially men like Lt. Victor Parks, Jr., and Capt. Allen F. Kingman, "officers and gentlemen" in the highest sense of the word. Upon the one or two officers of the other type it is quite unnecessary to dwell. When once free from contact with a skunk, one simply bathes, changes one's clothes, and promptly allows the odoriferous memory to be wafted away and disseminated in the ambient atmosphere of oblivion.

Silver bursts cut - Artillery flares at night show red, but in the early dawn they appear against the dark hillsides like bursts of silver.

Old Fusee

Fusee - Soldier term for his rifle, the French word "fusil" meaning that weapon.

The Colors of Blighty - Because of its brevity, succinctness and expressiveness, I have used the word Blighty to designate a military hospital, though it was never in really popular use by the American soldier for this purpose, and to the British soldier it simply meant going back to England, but as so often Tommy Atkins went back to his Tight Little Island because he was wounded, Blighty frequently meant "hospital."

When Nurse Comes In - The phraseology and repertoire of the army man must not be taken too seriously, as nine-tenths of the time it is simply a safety valve for ebullient spirits or dread monotony, and with little or no real harm back of it.

Charlie Chaplin in Blighty - The famous "movie" comedian of the cinema.

Embarkation Home

M P - Military Police; soldiers acting in that capacity.

www.ingramcontent.com/pod-product-compliance
Lightning Source LLC
Chambersburg PA
CBHW060055050426
42448CB00011B/2464